MW00453477

CoNMaNSiNiT
2023

STEPHEN W SWEIGART

Copyright © 2023 Stephen W Sweigart

Paperback: 978-1-960861-44-3
eBook: 978-1-960861-45-0
Library of Congress Control Number: 2023913377

All rights reserved. No part of this publication may be reproduced, distributed, or transmitted in any form or by any electronic or mechanical means, without the prior written permission of the publisher, except in the case of brief quotations embodied in critical reviews and certain other noncommercial uses permitted by copyright law.

SWEETSPIRE **LITERATURE**
—— MANAGEMENT ——

#1

Bib MiNenDezk (2006-2023 CoNmaN) New Jerzip

BeEn New Yr 1954 NyC, if ImMagruNt DeFexToR

fRim CUBA, Nit Fer Cub WoRErs, BuT DACA wOrKeeRs

ApoiT Bee Jea COrzInE 2006, feRgn ChAer

2013-2015 2021- pRES. DeAdLoCK BrIBeRy TrIaL

New FeD IVesTig cOrRuPTn. A Cap aTORny, RutGer,

DeVil PeTe, POliTic. ElEc Redis LAtiNos Too

CoNMeN Us, suPPoRt ReRubs. IvAde LyBA, SyRa,

OppOSe IRaQ invADes. ABorT FeTus, GaYMaRrig,

ImmGraTe REfir. Oops Bide adMin SeL TuRkEy, WaRPlan.

ALiCia daUGt oUTsPkEn fEmISt qUiEt faTHr sEx sCaNd

NSNBC COmTatR, sIn eLEC ConMan AlSo, NoPoolICAL NewLge.

16 olD seX fOr MeNy, DoMin ReP, MaNy TiMs.

FiBbeR investgig,

— *Bob Menendez*

#2

Mit McConN bin 1942, ALlimaba. Miv LooVIll,

GRad UnV Loovill 1964, HiSory. KeNtUc Law

KaRee PoLicS, AssAnt. sPorT baRgniG RIt puB EmPl.

Fun MemOr FoReSt. 1984, AScnT SeN. SiNc

ALm 40 yRs, DiKTaTor. AGist CAmPaiN reFroM,

On foR reLATn ComMit. SuPoRt iRaQ tRooP,

ReJEct WiTHdrAw. OPpOSse ObAMa.

AffOrDaBLe KaRe Act oPPeNt. KEEp GuAnTaN

DeTeNt OpEn. AgAiNt GuN CoNtroOl Bill.

dEbT LiM sPeND WaSt. MaJORy LeaDr Elec.

Boll tO adDrs OpIoID ePEC, AgRillCuLt.

BLoC SUPme COuRt nOMin, wIT TDump PrOM

RePeL OBaMa KaRe. FaL er InCeaS

oDD derRek RePubs. TAcX cUT PeRManT.

UPheAd SeX exEPm CoNmEn. WaLOvERtUr

paSS, $1,375 BiLlin. FRaC SHoWdEr.

SQus RuLs AdMd ImPeAch. FOgT AGst

CoVId $500 BiLLnon ReLeaF. BaPist, 35 mil NET.

— *Mitch McConnell*

#3

CoR BoOkUr, bin WASh DC, Ape 1969, AFfu PArEnts,

PrEstig EdUCot, STanD, YaL, Rayed NuRd JerZip,

RoaD ScOL, CiT CoUnL tO DoNk, deFat PRs, ProMiS

Bat KRim, pLoT AssiNaT oF Hm, OVrhAl PoLiCe.

bGAn PUB StUnTs: 10dy Hung Stk, PrIV PHilan,

ShOv DRivWy, FiR Sav woM, FaCeBook

100 million, From ZUKbG, on UoP WinPeY.

KarPoT BOggER, lARgEst PrOpErT InKREse.

100 mill PHiLanT fOr NeuArK, JoNT KamPanE 2012

SpOKeN Ae LaRGe KroWd, PaVwA PreSIdenT

Run. 2013 LAut dI, RN Sin AtE NJ, WeN, 2014, WeN.

2016 CLiTwOm SirT list Vp CAN, SPiK CoNveN.

DANgr EXpll Frm SIN aTe, iNtr KaVnOh EMaiL.

INtR LeGis RaCaiL iNEqUItY & RePraTn.

FeB1 2019, NoUNd PReS BiD, bUT LiTeL SuCCss.

DaTe AccTiRs RoS DaWsin.

— Cory Booker

#4

KiViNe MCaRtHe Jan 1965, BaKfL CA. BeeKaM

SpKer fLoPhuSe 2023. Pop aSsn FiRcHeF

Mm HuseKeP. FiX CaRs, AttN CoMm Collg,

WUn LoTty, oPeN Deli, DeRid Gov Reg,

bKam ReGn aDmiRor, Wok foR Bil ToMas,

Aftr SolD bUSn, rTuRn CollAg.

1992 AragE JuDi WaGs, HigScOl SwEehEaRt.

CA. Ung RePuBs, Nat FeD 1999-2001.

OarD KerN CoMm TuSt CoLge, thN CA.

AssMbL 2002. Thom infLn, FuNd RAsyng.

2006 Thom ReTiR, US Haus RepReseT.

StuD AlMak AmEr PoLit, fAmL ReLaT BUiLiNg.

2008 ReLeCk, COnSeR vICtoRs. 2009 dep WiP,

2010 WiP, CoAuTh Knw GeN CoNsev Ead.

2015 MaRd inFID, ND BoaTin UDErmnd Pop

HIl CliTwOm. WiThdrw fR SpEk. 2018 MinOr LeaD

Jan 6, 2021 reBuk DumP rOL, CoMm Sham PrOss.

2022 MId ELeC nO reD WaV, DEspt AfTr (19 CoNsr)

BLoK Hs SpEkShp. MTG hpl ELek SpkEr.

— *Kevin McCarthy*

#5

NaN PillOSeey (D'AsanDo) 1940, BaLd MaRlAn, FaM TrAd
PoLtiKs, FaTh CoNGrs, BRot Mayr. GraD TrIn CoLLg
1962. Et HusS PaU, 5 kiDs. Move SaN Fran CA
1987, diCtaTor EnT CoNgRas, SPoRt Health, HuMRiGt
1st Wom Spek Haus, OppSd IRAq WaR, dev beT
pAy jObs, Engy Policy ClEan. 2010 Puss
AffOr HeAtH. RiAn Chalg hr 2916 Min LeaD.
8 hR mArtHon dEFn DrEaMr, RoCrd siNc 1909.
2019 SpEak AgAgn, OppOs DuMp WaLL, gOvT sHuTdn
CaN StAtUnin AddRs, OvRtUn Nat EmErGy
FUnD ¼ WaLL, sHe aT OdDs prOgRsIv DeMos,
tHe SqUd, DuMp 1st Veto, wHo UnIt SqUD aNd PiLioSy.
ELet 4th TeTm Ass SpEKr. ImPeaCH DuMp,
WASte MoNy, TiMe BeT sPenT. PiLloOSy in BeD
UKRaiN, SiN RePubs nOt AllOw WiTnS, RiP uP
DuMp speech, Ass CoVid SpRed PaSs 2 triLl StIMlos
DuMp 'ViRiS' KallD, AfTeR 'StOrM KaPtoL'
AnTh ImPraCh TrIAl. ApoInT CHnY LiZerd, CoMiTy.
2022 ViSiTd TAiWn, HaTE ChINa, HeIGhT tenToN.

— *Nancy Pelosi*

RaF ToaD CrOz (1970) pOP ImPrIs BaPtsT, MiM

bIN DELaRe, BeeN ABerT CaNda, MoVd

HoZutuN TX, 1974. RaZ SuzTH BaPtISt, PRiNtuN

uNiVs, DiBaT TeM ChUmP, HaRvLaW.

ClErk FeR 4tH DiSk KoRt AppeL, 1995. tHEn fiR

JuS ReNqUst 96-97. 1997 PrIv LeGL PrACiS.

DiD WerK oN ImPEavh oF CLitMaN, oN BuSh LeGL

TEm, GoRe vs. BuSh SUPm CoUrt.

2003 SoLic GenaL, TX. CoNsTu LiTrAl, InT TrEay

CoNstUlLy !0 CoManDmts oN Pub Buldgn, pVt pRaCt

2012 1st eLeC poS CoNMaN, OPPnt PPACA

21 hr SPecH feSuLt GoVn ShUTdwN, dRSuZ.

2014 reNocN CaNdaDa CiTz, EnTN PrEs ElECton,

Smal GoV, LiMd AcCet ABoRtn, StaTe DesiD SaMsEx.

BeKme DuMp sUpPr, 2020 SuPot pRez LeCtoN.

CrOz FiLd NuMeRs ElEcTn COrT cAsEs. StUm CaPiTL.

– Ted Cruz

MaR sHt BLuNenBoRn (1952) bEn, Ne WeDgWerT,

lAuR MiSsp, SenTn 2018, fr TeNNsee. 2019-.

MaRd ChUk BlAck, SaL puBl, ReT FaShon DiRt,

1978, MaRk, Evnt MAgMnt, foNDed.

jOnt ReBuPs, CoUtn CHaiR, dElLg RePuBs,

1992 NaT CoNv. RaN unSUsiss US HauS RePs.

EkeRtaN InDuStr, 1995-97, TeNN MuSiK

ComMiSs. 1998, TeNnsis SeNtik. 2002 US HaUs

RePrSeTv, ElEcK. LaU CoNsT AmMend,

BAlnC BuDgt. TaX KuTs. AGiStn ABoT Rizgts.

OpPontn PLaNPaRenT. SuBCoMit EkerGy, CoMmeRs,

2016 EnDooSt DuMp. AfTr biB KooKr nIt

SiK ReLectn, 2018 rAn oN DuMp, Wion SiN CeAt.

mUsIk AcTk, VeTAffAr, cOnSUm PrOtCt, Prodi Safty.

BOokS, CoNServ WoMn, Lief Eqity. Cam vT.

— *Marsha Blackburn*

#8

M&MteeGee {1974} biN MiLlgeviL Ga. Hs s FoThYe,

UoFGeog, in hs 53 HelD hOSt, PeRcYGrzEn 1995

DiVoRs 2022. TayLo ComM, CoSFitgYm hrslF.

2016 RePuBs PrIm EleCts, WrT 59 ArTclE fER

'TrUTh SeEkr', CoNsPiR NeWsp, 27 ArztiC

LWa ENfoRc, fAkE nEwEs WeB. 2017 PrOtesT,

2018 FaMAmeRc PrOj, pOsTd TrEaTs

AgSnT DeMoS, ClAiMd gov CoMMe iNfLtzrat.

2919 vIseT CoNgRsT, oN FaCbk pOsT OuTsd OaSio-

KoRtEz. OMaR, TlAib, SweR QurAn, Nx MeMbs

2020 PrIM ElECts, beG CaMPgn 7rh Dis,

Latr 14th diS, BAlaNce BuFg, 2sd AMdMt

pOSt PhOTos APUSA KlaLiFf LeaDr. 1st uT RuNofF

AcCuSed FuNdng PPP. wOn rUN oFF.

GeNeRL ElECtiOn: HeVy ReBuPs DiStrik, Ar-15

RyfLr oN FaCybk, pHoTo SquAD, dELeTd GuNRiGts

RaLly, kaLlEd PsLOsyee bITcH, FrUd. 2022 eLeKtn

DoNuR uNdziSkOlsed, 14th AmDedMt' dFeTd FloWers.

— *Marjorie Taylor Greene*

9

MaRx WaRnErD {1954} bisMAn PoLtiC, {2002-06)

GoV ViRg, (2009--) SiNatE USa. BiN InDapOlS,

Ind. PuB SeXtAy ScHo, TeAch InSp PoLiC,

GrOg WaSH UNiV (1977) BA PoLiC ScIEn.

4.0 gRd AvG, wOk CaPhIl pAy TuziTon, in CoLLg

"I Se WHt HouSe whE PrZ" tOL pOp.

GRaDet HaRvd, lAW (1980). nEV PrAc LaUw

faILd 2 BuSiNs fOUnd, (80-82} jeB fUn RaIS DeMos.

maNG WiLers GuB cAmP (89). transport

ViRgnia BoAd, uNsCess Us SiN rUN, (2001).

rUN GUbneRd, RuLl sUpoR. 20 mil to 10 mil

OuT SpEnDt. (2002) dRw fr SuRpus.

VRGiNa voTR ReJecT SaLs TaX. TaX inCRes

1.5 BiLLn aNnly. DeNIde CLeMcy 11 DeAtH

SeNtSe. 2009—ElEct SiNteR, AmRc ReCozbll biL

2013 SeNir SiNr, PrO ChOic, 2019 MiNr AcT

2010 DoDd fRn Act, rLaX BaNkIn ReGuL. PrEvNt

FoRgn gOvs FR AdDs pYRch. VeTo AgN iSreL

SaCtn IRn, RuSsa, N KorA. EqUlAcT.

— *Mark Warner*

Kuk SchOeMaR (1950) bin, BRokly, NY. PerFSaCt

HaRvd BA PoLtiC 1971 LaU 1974, nOt PraCt.

1974 ELec Ste AssMbLy. 1980 MaRrdy 1981-1999

HauS RePtsREntvs, LiB, 1993 ViOlecEn PrEv

1994 HaNdgUn PreVtuN, baN Assault WEap.

PPACA PrOmOt, 2016 ELeC SiNaTe, VoCL OpPenT

DuMp, DeFt RePEL PPACA, ScHmAr defeat.

BiDeN poLiT rIVaL, 2019 HaUs ImPeCh DuMp,

McCon BlOcLk ScHueMaR, iNSiN.

2$ triL ReLeaf StaIM pAC, BiDn WuN 2020.

DuMp diSpUt ELecTn, StUm CaPtlL,

ScHuMaR AccURs oF InCiT

Majority LeAdr, oF SiN, HaUs ImPeCh VOt.

— *Chuck Schumer*

Stephen W Sweigart

MaRiELviRiSaLCzAr (1961) LiT HaVna biN, PaRNs

CuBN EXil, BiLiNg, PoR RiCo, mime DaD Colge

1983, BaC ArT, 1995 HaRv UnI, Ma. 1983 rePt, 1984

SpAn NeWs, 1988 rEpT WhTe HaUs, Pezntg.

1991 cHif Sozth MeRca, 1993 TeLmn, KuBa coRes

InTerVw FiDel KaStRo, 1996 PoLizt debate,

& kAnOSa. InTveW AcTr oF EsKoB, + LeWtEn JJ

VeLasSQue. FrM KiLan PreZ, AuSz PiNoChIo.

2013 deSsDeNt YoNi SaNzcIZ, 1999 CLiTmAn

2001 GwBuSh, mAmATeRsA eTc. FoX Nuzs

2018 AcNowcIDed KaNiDaTe, LoSt To ShAlal, pARtic

FrDuMb FoRc, Wn 2020 HaUs RePre ElEcTn.

CoVid qUaR, MisSd CeRtf EleCt ReSuTL, VoTAgsT

DuMp ImPeAchMt. vOteD ApRoV JaN 6,

CoMMity. oPoNenT tAx PaY Abort, Might ImMgr

CiTzshp, aNtITrUs FiSh MerGr BiL, VoT aGist

AmeRkn ReScUe pLaN, CaRbn TaX VoT, BaKgRn

Cos GuNs, vOt AgAsnT bAn Assault zweApOns. SoPoRt

ObAmA CaRe oNLy ALtErntv, SuPRt IsReL,

— *Maria Elvira Salazar*

DaB WaSsErtNaN SulHoLz (1966) biN QuINs Nyc, PoP

CpA, TiLl !978 LiDo BeCh, Lg Islnd. 1984 Hs in MeLvl

BA polit ScIen, & MaS, UnIV Fl. LiV neR Ft. LaUt

MaRg Stv SuHtz, AcTv Jw Nat DeMos, PlaN PaRenT

2009 SuGre BrEst CaNcR, PrMot EaRly ScRn.

1988 AiD sTAt LeGis, RaN StaT LEglaTr. 8 yrs TeM

LiMiT, Then tAUgt pOlit SciNc Comm CoLg. SerV SaTe

SIN ProM MaNiTe. 2004 CoNgRs, 2011 DeMo

ChIR NaT CoMMt. 2016 SkaNdEl WikILaKs EmALs

uNEthIC FaV CLizTwOm OvEr SaNdEs,

FuNdnG DbT. support GuN CoNtol, LGBT, KriTz

UkRain 2015 lAw GLorFy InSuRgt PaRty, pRO NaZiS,

VoTd ImPaCh DuMp, PrO IsReAli Kritz RePuBs.

JEwIS HeRiTg MoNtH, 2008 VoT EcOn ZtAbzaT AcT

During FiNcIL KrSIS. LeGiSLat AgAzt HaTe KrIMe.

AnT ChINeSe AcTiV, SoLtz. InKrees PeNaLy IDen TeFT.

AgAsT MeDiKal MaRina.   2017 CaP PoLiZe

AKcuRzd 5 StAFers sTeAl CoMpers, ScUltz did not

FiRe, 2016 scHed Oly 6 DebAteS, UnVit GaBrd 1st.

— *Debbie Wasserman Schultz*

═══════════════════

#13

AnOy kUm (1982) biN BoStiN KoReAn ImMGrNts
MaRtuN, NJ. MuV CheRy HolE, EaSt HS.
DeP Sprng, UnIV ChIAgO, 2004 PoLiT ScIcEn
MaGDaLn CoLge, OxFoRt. mEt PeT BuTiGey.
UaSs StAt DePTmt, AfGHan cIVlAn AdVisR
NaTSeCit AdViSr PrEs OBaMa. 2018 ELeCt deFt
RePub. EnDooRs OBam & MuRhy. ClOS Race.
2022 WuN ELeCt, StReNin HeAltH CaRE, StOp RaZe
oF ConGRas, VoTd CoN BiDEn 100%. CoVd SuB
CoMMity, JuStce PoLiCin, BaN 'trAd STocKs' CoNGraS.
CeRtFy PrEZ ELecTn, DoNteD Blu SuIT tO
SMiTsOn InStTud, inDo SuB CoMmiT, HuMaN
Rights, GoLB HeAlTh. iNTerNaT oRgAnzaT.
PrOgRsiVe CAUcus, AsIAn PaCiFiC AmErKn.

— Andy Kim

GoSh GoDdEnTiMaR (1975) LiVgnTuN, NJ.

pAgE SiN LaUTbRg, SiN Us SexTaRy, UofP

HaRv LaW, 1996 reELet CLiTmAn CaMpaIn,

peMbRk OxFert, MoDHiS. SpEEchWroT FeR

1998, JuN KeRy PrEs KaMpAin, HiTy CLiTWuM

WuKe FerD MoTr, 2010 FeDCoMuNKaT CoMm

StRaT MiKroKoSt, 2017 EleK CoNmAn, NeWJrZiP.

MoSt CoNsvtv DeMo, VoTd DuMp, NoW BeNdEn

PrOsD Salt, 2021 CeNt DeMo DeRaL InFrTStuC AcT

SyRiA ChEm WeaP, 2017 PrOB DuMp RuSsA

VoTd ImPEaH DuMp TwIc, FeR AssNaT IrAN GeNL,

VoT AgsT CaNnzbiS (MaRiJuNa} peN BaNk

iN iTs InDuStRy. ClOSe PoRts RuSaN EnErY.

RePdzc FiBbezr TaPe MLK. MaRd TuSk, 2 ChiKd.

— *Josh Gottheimer*

#15

rEbKa MiKiE ShEReaL {1972} Us NaV HeLop PiLoT,

AtToRny, FeD PrOsCutE, CoNWoM 2019.

DeMo. BeN AleXdRr, ViRgIa. BS NaVAcDme,

LoNdoN sChoL EcOmi, WoRlD HiSty. ArAbIC lAnG,

aMeRkn UiVs KAiRo. JuRs DoC GrgTwn 2007.

1994 H-3 SeeKig PizloT, RuSin PoLy OfFcR. LootTn.

LefT KiRjlnD eLlS FiRm, ASsDiStrk ATtoRny Us

NJ. 2017 ReEdis RaN ConGrSs, rASd 2.8 MiLLn.

2020 HeLpD bYe JoE BiDeN. 2022 ReDiSt WuN.

JoNd MoDCoNsEr CaUcUs. NeT VoT Pelosy

SpKR. VoTd ImPeAc DuMp, InQuIRy UKrAnE.

AgiN 2sd ImPeAcH vOt. BLuEDoG CoLiTin. SPacE.

sUbCOmMit InTeLdeNC, sPeShAL OpERtn.

EViRmoNt ChAr, tACtKsL AiRfoRc, LaN.

MaRiD 4 KhiDrn, kLaSmAt.

— *Mikie Sherrill*

#16

KaRloSe A GriMiNeZd (1954) BeN HaBnA, CuB.
FaMy ImGrT tO MiAmI. BA BaRy UnVt, 1993 HaRv
KeNnyd Scul GoVmt. JoNt FIRe DePt 1975,
1991 FIRe KiEf MiAmi SeRv tilL 2000. InTeRnAt
FIRe AsSoc, FeD EmGcy MaNgm. 2011 eLeC MAyR
CuT 50% SaLrY. 2017 DuMp OrDeRd
reVw Fed FuNiNg, FLgd. GRiM OrDd
CoOpEaTe WiT IcE. 2020 ELeC LiMIt BaLLt
DrUp BuX, SeN OuT MAiL bALoT LaTe.
MIAmi AmErAiR StAtm EaRly VoT sITe, GrIM
inTeRveN, nOt MeNiOnt LiSt oF VoT SitE.
2020 AsNoUZnC CoNMaN AtTeM. RAn PlAtfm
REaPeAl AfFoRdaBle ATc. support CLitWoMaN.
IN 2020 SuPoRt DuMp. MeMb UnFrEe FoRc
StRiPtee MTG CoMmiTe, VoT AGasT AmEcAn
ReSuE PlAn. DuMp ShUd nOT cONced ELeCtn
UnVoT CeRt PeNnsyl anD ArIZn ECtaL VoT.
VoT FiR InVEsTaTe JaN 6, sTm CaP. FaIRns AlL,
ViOlAce Against WuMeN aCt. 2021 BaKgrnN cKs GuN.

– Carlos A. Gimenez

#17

LaWuN Op BoZFeRt (1986) BuSWoMuN, GuN ActVst.

ReSrtRauNt ShOOterS GrIL, 2013-2022.

LoSt $143,000 2019, $226,000 2020,

RiFlE, CoLrAdO. SFaf Only KaRy GuNs.

KoNfrOnT BeTo O'Roke oVeR SeM AuToMaTk FiFLe.

BeN FL. MoVd KoLrAdO, AgE 12 yR. 2004, HS

BAbY. GED CeRGiFk 2020. fAmLy WeLfArE.

FiRsT ReGiSt DeMo, 2008 RePuB. AssMcKeeDs.

2007 AfTr MaRrY fILng NaTgAs DrILgn Co, MeMb

tEM bUiL PiPLiN. Opened ReStuAn 2013.

2017 80 Got FoOd pOiSniNg fR tEMp loKtIoN

ShOtErS gRiLl. PrOtESteD CoViD reSRiKtIOn.

2019 RaLli OPpOsE ReD FlAg LaWz, TAkE GuNS DeEm

TrErT. PoSd aS MeMb ThRe PeRcEnT MkiLiTa,

lArEr DeLeT TwEeT. BiD tO Bee CoNWuM. DeNiD

ConNTuiN PrOUd BoYs, QaNoN. PLedG

JuN FrEeDuM KaUcES. Kriti Omar, JiHAd.

OpPoSes GReEn dEaL, oPpOseS CoViD rEsTiOn.

— *Lauren Boebert*

StOvE SkaLicE (1965) boN NU OrLeaN, UnV LuAn

BS cl<pt ScI & PoLiTkLsCiNe. LSU AkAdiA

AmDiKn, AmEkn ITaLn ReNnZanC. 1999 Elec

StAtE HaUs, OppOs StELly PLaN lOwEr FoOd, UTiL,

RaSe InKoM Tax. 2007 StAtE SInIT.

2008 Run & Elec Us Haus ReP. 2010 rELec.

2012 diSMiSsd STsFeR fR LoBiSt, AfTr sTuD commit

pUBL RePoR cPpYrIGhT. 2013 ViOLenCe

Against WoMaN Act. 2017 fAvOr TaXkuT BiLl.

HiMseLF mAJoRiTy WhiP RePlCeMcKaRtHy.

2017 JUnE 14, ShOt PlAyGn BaSeBoy. WiT CoNGrass.

LiVinG in KaR ReSoDd To RePuBs iNhUzmIY.

2020 ELeKtn VoTd DeSeRtJFy BiDeN, Arz, PeNyv.

EmMiGrAt SuPrT DuMp. A+ NaTRif AssEs. OpP AfFdAb

HeAlTh KaRe AkT, aPPlAD TeX LaU.

OpPsis LeGgaLzTn MaRJwAn, DeNiEs ENviR-

Mnt ScIEn KLiMiT ShAgE. sAmE Ex MaRiG Against

— *Steve Scalise*

Stephen W Sweigart

TiNy TiM EuG SkOTes (1965) Bon SUth CaRLin
PaReN DiVorC, RaSeD MuM poVtY. 1983-84 PrEStyiN CoLg
football pArT ColaRshiP. 1988 BS PoliTc SINc
ChRLsTn SoUtrN UnVty. WrK InSuRn. OwNc AlLsT
AgEnCy. ElEKon CArLsN CiTy KoUnCiL
1995. LoSt TaTe SiNtit 1996. rELeK CiTi KoUzil.
diFfr Dpt JuSt LuSeWt, 2001, VoT RiGts.
2008, SC hAus Reprst StATe ELektd. AgsT HiGh TaX.
2010 ElekT USA HaUs ReprSt. 2012 RePeA ELecTD,
DeNy JoNt BlK CaUs, DeNi FoOd Smpt in LaB StIKE.
2011 iNtRod leGIstlAt AgAst NRLB, LoKt BuSnEs.
SuCcsfLy AvKad DeGng $300mil. CaRstn HaRb.
dEBt SeIlinG dIViN InSpAtn bY PrAyeR,
KoNst AMDendMT. 2012 aPpInt bY GoVnerd HaiLy.
2014 siGD SuPt Rn JnSoN ChAlnG OFiC Pern
MaNgmT RuLg AFfoRd KaR AkT. 2016 LyChg FeD HaT KriM
2016 VoTd aGnt PrVt PaRtshaL GoV ShUDn.
AnD SpEnD $1,375BIL WaLL MExCo BoRd.
2021 DeLiVd RePuB reSpNs tO PreS BiDeN AdRs CoN.

– Tim Scott

#20

JoNg KiNN (1962) bin Repub, assemb 2114-16, 2018
LoS CoNgr RaC, 2020 WoN CoNgrwOm. Bin S.
KorA, tHeN GuAm, tHn HaWAi HS. GrAd
BuSn AdM UnIV S. CaLiFoRNiA. FiSt FiNac BnK
SpOrT MaNuF, SELf EmPly ClOthng. Work
EdRoYc StAt SiNtr, 21 yRs. RaDiO SUol, discus PoLTc.
2014 ELec StAt AsSmb, DeFeAd 2016. 2018 AfTr
RoYc rETiR, KiNN acUnCd CoNWomn Run
LoSEs KlAm FrUd, FiNNy ConCed.
2020 RUnAgIn WuN. iN 2021 VOt SerRtiFy BideN
VOt aGst iMpICmt oF DuMp. VoT SRiP MTG
oF GoNgEs KoMmty, VoT AgIStN EQuAiTy AkT.
Against AMerkaN rEsKum PlAn 2021.
VoT FiR ViOLnS WuMEn aKT, AgSt DeLy SoC
SeKuRt KuTs. vOt RePub KauKus 96%. PrEs BiDeN
31% VoTd. OPoSiTsn AFfoRb KaRe Act.
SuPpOrT PoLiCe, AkKunTaBiLy, TrAiNinG.
kOnSeRn KoRean SpliT fMies. NoRt & SoUh KoRe
OpPse SaMSeX MaRrAg, LGTB nO TrAn WuMaN SPoRt

— *Young Kim*

#21

THuM HoW CaiN Jr. (1968) Fr 2001-03 GeN AsSmBy
NJ, 2003-22 Nj SiNte, 2008 MiN LeAd NJ SiN.
ChRiStiE tRiEd to ReMoV, FaiLd.
2002—USA CoNMaN. 2000 FaiLd, 2020 LsT
To DeMo, 2022 DeFate DeMo. SiN of Tm Cain Gov
oF New Jerzip, 1982-1990. FaMly EarL SeTlers
MnY pOliTcs LeAdeRs. GrAd DaRMot CoLge, LuW &
DipLoW. TufT UnVeR, DoK InTrnAt StUd.
FiR FiGteR, UnD BuSh EnViR PrOtEct AgEnY.
iN New Jerzip SiN, SrEam Gov., EvIrNmt,
LoWr PrOpy taX.
2006 LoSt tO DeMo MeNenz, USA SiN.
2022 MiN LeaDr USA CoNMaN McKart EnDoRsD.
BAtE DeMo, USA CoNMaN ElEkTn.
RePuB MAiN St PaRtshP. PrOb SoLv, KriTiz
nOt mOr DisT DuMp. EpISkoPalLin.

— Tom Kean Jr.

#22

JiF VoN BrEw   (1953) bin PoLitsAn & DeNst ,

SeRv CoNMaN New JerZip, USA. 2019 DeMo –

2020 RePuB. MAyoR, FreEhOlDr,

GeN ASseMbLy (2002-08), SiN Nj (2008-18)

BiN NyC, GrAd RuTgR UnIV, DmD FairDiCk UNiV.

NJ SiN CoMn UrBaN AfFar, MiLtry VeT AfF

SpOn FaIR DrUg PRiCiNg Rx aRd. cOmM HaUs AfFoD.

2018 StAt LAgeSt CoNMaN diStrCt.

2020 AgiaNsT DuMps ImPeAcHmEt, DrOpd Fr

BLuE DoG KoLiTn, diStRiK LeAn RePuB. sWitCH PaRTy

Fr DeMom tO RePuB. 2022 ReELekiPn.

fiRsT DeMo rEPrSenT diStRkt SiNsE 1995.

CaMpAiN VoT Against PEloSi, VoT against

ImpEAchMT of DuMp, VoT Against zreMovInG

MTG. VoTd OuSt Liz ChEnY fR CoNGrAs

VoTd FoR InFrAsTuRuRe Akt & JoB AkT.

2021 VoTd fOr NaTnaL DeFeNsE AtK, AlLiEs AkT,

vOtD Against h r 7691 aDiTonAl FuNd UKrain.

CoSpOn FaIRneSs Akt, SaMSeX Marriage.

— Jeff Van Drew

KrS SmTh (1953) 1980-PReCenT RePuB CoNMaN

New Jerzip. 21 TErmS. HOmaN RitEs AbUSe.

TreNTon State grAd, LoSt tO frk ThOmp iN 1978.

1980 ThOmp INdiCtd AbSCaM, SmTh WuN,

CoNMaN sEaT. !982 MeLiNo "BeAt It KiD". T SmT

1984-PrEstn DeFeT OpPeNt bY 60% oF VoT.

Co-SpONcr ImPeAcH CLiTMaN 1997 pReDaT 1998

LeWiNSky SaNDeL ImPeAcHmt ATtEMpt

2015 inTeRn ReVeAl qUeStN aNsWeRd, pErSn,

OrGanzaT. DeLgAte UN TwCe.

VoT AgSt ImPEac DuMp, TwIC.

2021 VoT StRiP MTG Of Co.Mmty. VoT Fer

InFrAstrUct InVmt & JoB AcT.

SuPpoRt VeTrAnS, ReMovT frM ChAiR VeT

bY RePuBs, NoT FoLiNg BudGt. 2014 MeGaN LaW iNt

2020 VoT DuMp 3Rd LoWeSt.

BaKGrNd ChEk 2021, vOt FeR.

– *Chris Smith*

#24

HarLaNd 'AnD' BaERr (1973) biN LeXtiN, KeNTuK.

SeRvNg 2013— CoNMaN. Family oLd LeXtiN.

BarR StReEt, Pop AcCoUn FiR & PhYcIn PrAciC,

MaM DeKoN EsPiKaL DiSOS iF KeNtUk.

uNiV ViRgiN, kOnTrB KonSerV ViRgizn AdVokt,

InTerN MiTSH McKonNL, GrAd GoV & PhiLsO, BA.

1996-1998 lEgiSaT AsStAnt, J. TaLnT, MiSoRi

2001 JD fR UnIV KenTuk LaU. NoNpRoFizt ChRtY.

StiTs & HaRbiNsn, BuSsiNs LiTgAtn. GuB KNdaT FleCt

hIRd HiM DeFenD RuNninG MaTe. FaILed DeFen.

FleCtr TeRm MaRrd HiRg SkAnDel, ExEcTv rEsIGn jOiN

BaR DiRktOr, BaRr beKAm GeNrL CoUnCil..

DeFeNDeD PlAcEm oF 10 KoManDs, stAT KaPtAl.

FleCtR DeFeAD 2007. 2010 DeFd bY DeMo

CoNMaN, BaRr KoNteSd Result. 2012 BaRr WuN.

2014, 2016, 2018, 2020, ReLeKtD. HaUs KoMm FiNcn

NaT SeKurty, MoNtArY Policy. MiliTaRy SAVE,

87MlL HEAL FiR KuNtuK, OpEoSd. CAROL AkT;

2023 InTrOdc HJ Res30 BloCk ESG iN reTiRe VeTroN

Bi BiDeN.

— Andy Barr

#25

BrHaNDadY WiLLamBs (1967) Bin DaLass Tx.

BA PePpdinne UniV, MBA Wart Schol BuS

USA nAvY NuClr SuBmirn, Ko FoUnD CPLANE.ai

SoFtwAr CompY. ELeKd AfTeR DisTrk DiVdd

US HaUs RePrsnt, 2022. YeA, DeNunC SoCiAliSt.

OwNs BeE FaRm, with StePHaniE, WIF.

— *Brandon Williams*

NiKoLd MaLeOiStAKe (1980) USA HaUs RePrsT 2021
biN MaNhTn, MoVd StAtn iS, ImMgRnT pAr Pop
GreEse, MuM LeFt 1959 CuBa. BA SeaTon HL
MBA WaGnEr. Wuk StaT Sen 2003-04, GoV paTki
2004-2006, StT EnGy zcoN EdSon, PuB AfiR.
2015 MaRco RuBiO Nam HeR Ny ChIr hS cAmpgN
2010 Elec Stat Sin. 2011 AmeR AuTo AsS LuwSuiT
AgNisT Ny PeRt AuThoty, toLL rAiSe, HaRdShP.
2012 reELct. FogT KeP SenoR ceNtOr oPeN.
ForMu MTA PaYrll Tax, ImPCaT sML BuSinSs.
FoUgT ToLl inKreS, ImPk am busS. 20117 MayOrRc
LoS INcBint deBlas. 2020 RaN USA HaUs ReP.
ShE bAcKd DuMp, He InTuRn SuPpOrTd hEr. ViCtoRy.
2022 RePeAt. 2021 TrAnSprT KomMty.
VotD to SuSpnD MTG. VotD fOr InFrSsTuRe JoBs
AkT. jaN 2023 sIt oN HaUs wAyS MeAn
KoNseRv CLimiTe KaUkuS, TaIWaN KaUhUs.

— Nicole Malliotakis

VikToR KuLhEyKo SpAz (1978) bin UkRaiN (USSR)
BS MBA KyiV NaTn EcOnOiK UnIV. ImMgRt USA
2000, CiTz 2006, MaStr AcCoNtcY, KeLy
Bus – PuRdu. FoUdnG TeA PaRty, cfO InDiAn
AtToRny GeNrl. OwNs ReAlst & FarM BuSn.
2020 InCumB nT ReEeK, rUn US CoNWuN, SuPoRt
DuMp. WuN. 2022 DeFt DeMo. fReDoOm FoRse
HiGh StAf TuRnOvr ToXiK EnViRnmT. KaL StaF 'M'RaN'
VoTd miXd 2023 HaUs SpEaKt. Feb. 1 2023
NoT SeK ReLeCtn. Or Any oFfSe. RuScHn InVaSn
GeNoSd, bUt KrItC oF ZeLnSkyY, & YeRmk. vISt TwisE
During WaR. SuM MeMbs CoNGras saYs
HeLps RuSsA by KriTcziM. Fr AbAsSd dISKri AcK-
UsAtiOn, DiSKrt bY UkRaNn FoRgn MisTr.
AnTi-KoMptiOn HoSpItAL BiLl, Anti-SoCLiSt, Bg GoVm.

– Victoria Spartz

28 ———————————

TiM WaLLBuRgeR (1951) GrAnPaRnts SwEdIS.

biN ChICaG, ThoR FrCAc Nrth HS. MicH HaUs

ReP 1983-1998. 2004 LosT RePuB PrIM

USA HaUs ReP. 2006 DeFt DeSpt ReKaL.

2008 DeFt by DeMo, OnE lArgeSt SpeN KaMpAgN.

2010 DeFtd DeMo. 2012, 2014, 2016, 2018, 2020

AgAn DeFt DeMoS. AgISt BeLiV Klimt ChNg.

"E BeLiV iN gOd wHo IS BiGgR tHaN Us, E KoNfiDnT

IF ReAl PrOBleM, hE WiL tAkE KaRe oF iT".

AgNsT AfFoRdBe KaRe Akt. ChArE oFfSe WiTH

JaKsOn RiGtLiF. VaNDeLzeDd. 2022.

Ko br CaM CeX MaRrAg bAn biL.

2008 bITh ThEry PrES ObAMA ImPaCh, 2020

nE oF 126 RePuBs siGnd sUpPt lUwSuT

kOnTeSt PReSdEnT ElEctIOn ReCulTs.

OrDaIN PaStEr aS BaPtIsT, bUt nOn dOmINaSiOn

SuRcH oF UnITed BrEtHRn of XhRSt

— *Tim Walberg*

———————————

BiB GaaD (1965) Mov To ViRgiNa aT 9, BS FiNAnc,

MaSteR Busn AdMin, LiBrty XtaiN AkAdemY.

17 yRs CiTi FinAsaaL, 2016-2019 CaMbEL CoUNty

BoArD oF SupErVis. aGaNst SaM CeX mArG,

2sd aDmEnt Right. 2020 aLiGn DuMp,

FaR riGHit viEWs, AgAinSt MaSks & CoVd policy.

DeFt DeMo PhySiaN. 2021 vOTd aGainS

SeRtiFy ElEcTnn, eMbRSed CoNspry ELecT tHeRy.

'hOaX' mThoDs pReVnT CoVd. rPeaL AUMF iRaQ.

VoTd AgAigT ALLId AcT. VoTd AgAsT

NaTnaL DeFSiFe AcT. MuSst fOLloW 'GoD's Luw'

DoMsT vIOlnCe LeGiSltIOn. bOyKot KaP Kub

bEkAaUs oF VaSInE ReQuiRmTs. VotD aGaNtS

FiLnG FeE MoDeRaZaSiOn AcT: aNt-TrUsT.

eFfOrT ImPeCh PrEs BiDeN, & sEcRtRy HoM lAnD SeC.

ReMv TrOps fR SyRa, H Kon Res 21.

EiMnAte PrAkTicAl TrNiNg Przogm EliMnAte

FoRgn GraDs wOrK in US.

— Bob Good

#30

AnT D'EssPoSsdTO (1982) rEtRid PoLicE DTeKtIV
RePuB uPSseT CoNMaN ElzeKtIOn. MiLaRy,
JoINt NYPD 2006-2020. 4 KomPLaNts ExsSiVev FoRsE
AlSo StriPpeD VaKaTioN 15 WorKinG as DJ, ALiKi
SeRvINg. DoKtD 20 dAys VaKaTiN fReArM
StOlIn LeFt in KaR uNinteNd. ApPoINtd HeMpStd
TwN KoNSiL. 2016 FuLl TeRm tILl 2023. ELeCtd DeFt
CaMpAin PuzbLik SaFty, KoSt oF IviNg.
Kalld for Fel RePuB SanTs tO rEsIGn. FoRtuN FrUd Ak
inTRod leGiSLtn. SuPpoRt McKaRty SpeAkr.
VoTd AgAiNsT H Con Res 21. wHicH reMoV
TrOoP SyRiA.

— *Anthony D'Esposiito*

MiCHaiL ViNSeNt LaWLaRe (1986) RaKLaNd CoUty,

BS AkkOuNtgn FuNaNsE, MaNhAtiN KoLlg.

PaRtNerD KomMiKatIOn ChEkMTe Strategies.

AdViCoR tO ExCuTve DiRekToR RePuB PArtY, Work

DePtng ToWn SuPrVicor oRngEtoWwn, NY.

RePuB KaNdAt US hAuS RePCenT. WuN 2022.

KalleD SNtOs ResIN, UnIFy beHNd

McKArty hIS StAtMen, DeFuNK IRS aS AllOk

InFaTiN ReDutIOn Ak. ReInTroD wIT

GoDmIRe, AnTiKontIOn TaX Ak. VkTd tO

ReMv ihAn OmAr fr Frgn AfFrs KomMt.

VoT aGnSt PaRntS BiLl of RiGhts. AdMeN wNt To FaR.

— *Mike Lawler*

SKooTt GoRedOne PeRrY (1962) ReTr US NaTioNaL
GuArD BriG GeNrL. 2021 ChAiR FeeDumB KaCuS.
2sd AmdmNt KaCuS, JaN 6th KomMity SuBp
DeKinE, SitINg LeGL ReAsN. ReFR EtHIc PaNL.
GraNdSuN CoLuMbn ImMgRnT, Bin SaN DeAgO, At 7
SenTrL PinSiLvaNiVaNa, Family PuBLiK ASsiTaNcE
VoTeCh ScHL, AsSiSaT HaRriSbG KOmMitty
KoLgE, BS BuSneS AmIN, PeNn StTe. MaStR Degr
iN StRtiGiK PaNninG, US ArMy WaR KoLiGe.
1st JoB piK FrUit, MeChnik, dRaFtmEn, InSuRanCe
AgEnT. MaRRd ChRiSy, CHildrn. PrOTes
1980 enTrd PenN NaTLGuRd. GrAd OfFsEr.
HeLokpER PiOlt, 2002-03 BoSna, HerZgoVnA.
2009-2010 OpERtn IRaQi FreDMb, 1400
mISsN, 44 KoMbTMiSsn. PrOmTd KoLnaL. BrIG GeNr
ReTiR 2019. 2002 PeNn DePt EvIRmnT ProTeC
BrOUgt KrImiNL ChARge FiR AlTriNg fAlSfY
ReKoR Sewr. PeNn HauS RePrsT, 2006-12. 2012-
2022 US HaUs RePr. KeEp TrooPs AfGhisTn.

– *Scott Perry*

#33

AnA PauLoNa LeWnA (1989) Mexkan-Amerk, ParEn
NeV MaRrd, MuM maRrd AgAin. 2009-2014 AiR
FoRsE, airfield management. 2013 ApPeRd
'Hot ClicKs'. BrEf in StRip KluB. DeGrE BiOloGy
WeSt FloRiDe UnVsty. diReKtOr HiSpaN eNgAgMnT
TuRnInG PoINt. On FoX nEwS cOmPrE HiL CLiTw
tO HeRpEs, cUt ShOrT, HoSt ApOlgIzE.
VP oF BeNvEnTo, CoRrEPoD ConSeV DiGiTL
MeDiA. 2020 EleCtN, LoSt GeNrL EleCt
US HaUs RePrsTn. HUsBAnd, hEr St PetEbUg,
nEAr AiRbaE. 2022 ELeCd, bEfoRe PrIMaRy
oNE RePuB WaNtEd hEr AsSiNaTd. eNdoRsd bY
DuMp and MTG wBo CaMpAiGn fOr HeR.
2023 VOTd AgAiSt McKarY fOr SpEAkr, NoMinAtnG
JiM JoRnD, tHeN ByRn DoNAldS.
FrEeDuB KaUkuS. 2020 VotEr FrUaD ELecTn.
AbOrTn BaN, NiT CeLl GAs tO Other NaTn, OpPsd,
GeN ThEry, AR-15 PiN oN LaPL. ReMv TrOop
SyRa, & SoMala, SuPoT EnDn KoNflt UkRiN.

— *Anna Paulna Luna*

MaRKoN RuBCoN (1971) CuBaNAMer, Bin MyAmi, FL.
PaReNts LeFt 1956, BeFr CaStrO, MoTh return iN
1961, oF 4 TrIPs. NaTriz 1975, aftR reTn. He StTd ThEy
LefT DurinG CoMmist. 1993 BA UnIV FL.
PoLiT ScINc. Doc LaW MyMi ScH Law. InTeRn
US HaUs ReP. iN 2000, WuN FL HAuS ReP. ModErT.
rELeCt 2002, 2004, 2006. LeGiSlaT SeSn 60 dAyS.
PraCt LaW fIRm LaNd UsE ZoNiNG. 2005 BeKm SpEak
BoOk 100 IdEaS, 24 laWs. 2006 CrISt GoVn
RuB KlAShd FrEqlY. TaX CuT biLl, LoWr PrOpErY
RaiSe SAlEsTAx; As ApPnt PrOfEsT FIU, FeLw
wHLe LAyOfFs aS HaUsReP FuNdeD FIU. 2010 US SiN
fUn RaISe, DeFEt KRIsT. 2016 RAn PrEs, LoSt
ReLeC SiN. 2022 rELetD, EmBaRgo AgAiSt KuBa.
MiLiTaRy KaMpaiG aGaISt LiBia, VoTd AgAiNst BuDgt
KoNtRoL AxT. WiTh SiN KooNs AmeR Growh
ReKoVry Act. RePleAl ObAmA Kare, Against BacK
GroNd CkS FiR GuNs. AGNst PuLbSh RePoRt oN CIA
TorTuRe, AbCenT 2015 35% SiN. VoT AgAst Jan 6.

— Marco Rubio

#35

ABjAiL AnA SpOnBUrGiK (1979) BiN NJ, 13 MoV
Shrt PuMp VA, pAgE US SiN, BA UniV VA.
MA BuSns AdMiN. 2002-03 sUbStdE TeAch
iN IsLaMc SAudI AkAdMy, eAr 2000 PoSt
InSpKtOr, 2006 JoNd CIA, ApPiOnt FAiR HaUsg
2018 DeCIDeD tO RuN FiR US HaUS of rEPreCt,
AfT RepuBs VoTd tO RePeAl AfFoRD KaRE Akt,
InKuMbNt TeA PArTy Member, DEfeAtD.
2020 WuN bY sMaL MaRgN, sH KrITzd DeMo StRdGy
WaTc aDs oF RePuBs, NeVr uSe wOd 'SoCAliSm'
oR 'DeFuNd PoLiC'. pHoN kaL LrAkd.
PeLoSeE dISpUtd, SaYInG 'TlAiB' haD wUn
ALeSaDr oSaCiO-koRteZ nO SoCiALiSt KamPnD LoSt.
2022 KoS RAsE WuN rELeSiN. VoTd AgAiSt PeLos
AbOrTn, VoTd LiFt VaCciN ManDt fIR wOrkrs
StIF oN KrIMe SeNtNeS. KrTcizD DuMp
TaX CuTs fOr CoRpOraNtn. SuPprT USMCA
TraDe DeAls. KiMtE ChAg ThReAT. BaN
StOcK TrAd oF KonGraSmnwn. VoT BiDn 100%.

– Abigail Spanberger

#36

RuKi ZcOTt (1952) bN BloOm IL. AtTn CoMniTy CoL

EnLiStd in 1970 NaVy, RaDarMn. GI BiLl

GrD UnV MiSsOri, BS BuSiNesAdMin. jUiS Dr

SoUth MeThd Univ. 1978. WrK DoNShp

PrAc LaU TX. WtH KaPit & PArTnr PurShd HoSpiT

nEW CoLmbIA HoSpT. LAtrR PurCh

BaSc HoSpt, tHn GAlEn 1993 3.4 BiLLn, 90 HoSpt

ThN HosPt CoRpRtn AmErk, nOw LaRgisT HeAlTh KaRe

FrUaD iNvEsTgAt, CoLmBiA/HCA 14 cOuNt

FeLoNy, 600 MiL FinE. Civil SuiTes 2 BiLL sEtLe.

EcT. EcT....SpeNt 4.7 MilL Tv RaDio Ads PrIMrY,

GoV ELeKtN DisMiS SAiD FBI nEvR tRgeT hiM.

9SpEnT 75MiLI oN ElEcTn, 45 th GiVrN FL. 2014

ReLeKtn sPnT 83 MiL, oN CaMpn. HuRrKaN IrMa

EvCake uNeMplyM, TaXpaYr DeBt, KriMe

deKrEaSed. RedUcd FL EnViR ProTeCt. FuNd

EveRgraDe,i DeAtH PeNtMoRe ExIKuToN, DrUg ScRn

WELfArE. 2018 US SiNiT DuMp BuILd WAL,

WaRnt wEB SeArCh, aGaistt KoMmiSn JaN 6 riOt.

— *Rick Scott*

#37

CHoS EuG 'CHoP' rOy (1972) bIN Beth's, MA.

RaIsE LoVeT, VA. 1994 BS CoMmeRSe uzniV VA.

2003 UnIV TX LaU JurdR. bGaN WoKe AtTorny

GeNrl 2002 KaMpGn US SiNiT, AdviSe InTecT prOpty

KriMe, IMigRaTon. 2010 wOkE AnTrNy GeNrl

GovNor TX GoStWrIT, nOmnAt StAtE-

FED RElatIoN. 2011 diAGnoSt HogIN LymP

2012 SiN CrUz StAf, RePeL ObAm KaRe

AsStAt AtToRy GeN 2014. ThEn resign OR fIReD.

CrUZ PAC for PrES KaPigN, qUeSt DuMp KoNseRvtIIV.

2018, RaN US HaUs reP. WuN reELec

2020, 2022. JoIN FrEdUmB KaUkUs, SuPpoRt PuLl

oUt NATO, Against giving BaCk 800,000 to FeD

WuKerS fiR sHuTdN. HuRKaNe FunDs.

"wE HoVen Te DIStOy eLeCr CoLeGe" 2020 ELectn

rOy DeFenDd ToAd CrUz aGaINsT OcaSiO-KoR.

oBjEcTn PrOSedUrE 2021. SupPOrT leZ ChEny sTrP

HiR PoStn, bUt DuMp pErSoNL AttKs nIT pRdKiv.

OpPsD bill fiR CoMmSn JaN. 6. AgAiNt AnTi-LyNcHiG.

– Chip Roy

#38

KhRuSty MaR WhoLAhAnD (1967) ChdHooD NaVL BaS
PoP bIN KyiV, UkRaIN. LeFt EsKp HoLOkOsT.
BA StAnFeRd, EnGiNeRnG. AFROTC ShKoloRShP.
MA iN TeCH, & PoLiCy fR MIT. ActIV DuTy
AiRFoRc Base, BeDfoRd, MA. 3 yrs. SpAc & AiR
DeFcE TeChNoGs. JOiN AcTv ReCeRv 1991.
2004 aS KaPtiN EnD CerVIsE. ChIf oPeRaT OfFiC
SpOrTwAr. Need EdUKaTon System,
EnTrd U oF P re-ToK hARd CiEnSe, taught 11th GrDE
IN HiGh CoHoL PhILldeLa. JoIn SpRiNgBr KoLaB
tHEn CFO/COD. Left PoLitK KarEra.
2018 RuN KoNWu, aS ReCuKt MaRcH foR WuMon
2017 oEgAniz Bus TrIP. district ReDuStikTd
RePub puLLd ouT, eAsiLy wUn, KaMpAin fUnd
5 MiL. plaTfRm 'LiBtaL', 2020 ReELct
SenT leiTtEr to BiDen sEnD F-16 FiGt JETs
tO UkRain. NegTate pRisEs DrUG MaNfakor,
AgaInSt ONE paYer HeAlTh System.
OpPoS wiThDrw tRooPs SyEiA. LGBT in MiLtRy.

— *Chrissy Houlahan*

#39

TuMb BiRaNT KuTiN (1977) FaTh DisC sUpV dEpT
HeAlTh MoTh PrInc MiD ScHoL, gReW uP CaTL
FaRm. 1995 HaRvrd CoLig, PoliTiK ScIEnC
THesIS FeDreSt PaPiR. 1998 KlAreMnT GrAd ScH
EnTd HaRv LaU ScHoo. PrAC LaU. eNLiSt US ArM 2005
2006 OprAtn IrAqi FrEdUmB, lEd AiR assault
2008-2009 AfGhiSTaN kOnTr InSuRjenT & rEKoNsTuk
2006 WruTe LettEr NY TimEs, NeV pUbl
AKuSing JoUrN oF VIOlAtE eSpiOn LaUs. PuBL
KoNSeRv JoUrN. RaNgR CoNtRoVy.
2012 ELeKd US HaUs ReP, OpPnEnt OBaM
BiLLs, MoSt. 2014 RaN fiR SiNiT, aS SiNtOr ReCeivEd
DeTH ThReAthS. 2020 dEfeAd LizbeRtAriN
nO DeMos rUnNinG, outperform DumP.
BLoCLeD AmBaSsiTor ApPoiNmTs.
DuMp'S support, UnDeRstD nEeD To ShAtTr WaShnG
ElItE. SuPoRt 'WaTeRBoArdnG', wItH DuMp.
2016 reFuSd tO koNsIdEr OBaM SuPRm CoRt NoMinE.
AgAiNst PrISoN ReForM, Saying nIT iNKaRcErAte.

— Tom Cotton

#40

JoN NiKooLs BoOsEmEn (1950) brN LoUiSaNa,
rEtrN ArKsW, rAiSd Bro. UnIV ArKsW, LaTr
CoLige OpTomTry, 1977 co- CiNiC OpTomTry,
LoW & BliNd EyE sErVseRvs, aLSo.
2002-2010 US HauS ReP. 2002 IrAq ReSoLutn
2011 4500 USA died, hUnDs ThOuS CiviLaNs, sAid
"SucCes SaFe HaVn fOr DeMocRcY"
2003 DrUg FrEe AmeRcA, ExPaNd PeNaltys IN CoUrTs.
VeTeRn EkOnOmiK ChAiR. mEmB NATO PA.
2010 ELct US SiNiT 2016 & 2022. Votd iNiTLly nO
tO ELecTaL cOLaGe kOuNt, AfTr RoiTs ApPrV
TAx cUts tCHes, pRINIvcPLs iN LoWinKomE scHoOLs.
UpPoSe aBoRtiOn. AdDed To HistOr TaILs
BuTTerOvRLanD tRaIL. AgAjsT AfFrDaBle KaRe Ak
A Rate NaTnL RiFiL AsSo. VoT AgAnsT NoDiKriM Sex
For EmPLyRs, & Pay. AgAnsT DisABiLty KoNv RgT
VoT AgsT ViOLnt WumEn (triBaL CouTt)
ReSevs $150,000 fr OiL, CoAl , AgaSt PariS AcCoRd.
CosPn IsReAl BoyKot AcT. SuPpRt RuSan SaCtons.

— John Boozman

#41

JaM ELro RiSch (1943) 2008-2020 US SiNiT reElEt

uNiV Wis-MilWak & IdAho BS ForResTy

JD LaU. EnTD poLTks AdA koNt PRosk AtTonY

TauGt kRizm JuStc, MiLiNare TriAL SeRv.

1974 ELek IDaHoe SiNIT, 1988 DeFeTeD, aPpont 1995

2003-2006 LuTen GoVnr, 2006-2007 GoVnR

ProPrty Tax AkT 2006. LuTn GoVn 2007-2009.

2008 US SiNiT, reELt 2014, 2020.

LeTtr 22 SiNtoRs WiThRwL PaRiS AgRemnT.

BLokd HoLKoSt HisToRn LiPstAdt MonTr, KoMbt

AnTSeMtiSm. QuITe DeSeNt KhAgGogi kiLLg

AnT-BoYkt IsREal AkT. Prevent ReSurg ISIS aKt

2019 iNtENd pUnsH TuRky. EthIOpA saCTns

AnTi AbOrTn, RoMaN CAthOk, gUN RiGhTs, Against

BaKgRn Cks. OpPoS FiRst StEp Akt. aBsTaIn KaPit

RiOt committee KrEaTe, AgAsT ToXiC Akt FiR BnfT VeT

– Jim Risch

#42 ————————

RuN HaRd JoNsOoN (1955) BiN MinNsoDa. NorW
GerMaN deSnt. WukE vArIOs JoBs. BA UniV
MinNosOdA. BuSsn & AkKontng, 1979
MoVd oSHkoS WiSKonSn, Family PaStiK PACUR
SolD to BoWaTr InD. ReMaiN CEO, 1997
puRcHsd fr reMaInD CEO. ELeKd SiNiT WiScOn
2010 AgaiSt AmRiCaN reCoVry Akt, ReINves
Akt 2009. In 2010 SolD LiQd AsSeTs, in BLinD trSt.
2016 reLeKtEd. 2022 WuN Wit 50.4%
2022 MaRKt deCiDe WaGes. ReJEctS 'KliMaTe
ChAngE', "BuLlSHit" "KrZy". Blok EPA rUleS caRboN
EmISsoN. "KliMaTe AlwAys ChAgeS"
fiScUL Hawk 'SpeNd KutS'. ObMa tErM. DeBt SeiL
'OuTrGe' KloSed TaZlKs oN SS & Salary SoLdrs. DuMp
TaX KuTs fOr HiS CaMpAin dONarS. SoCAL Security
'PoNzi SChEm'. Gun LaW nO 'teACh VaLu' iN ScH
OpPseS AfFoRdbLe HeALh KaRe Akt. BLaM
SiNiT McKaNe. AnT AbOrT. EliM StEm CeL EmBry
CoVid 'Mor DiE on HigHwy' SHuT Dwn EKonMy. eTc.

— *Ron Johnson*

#43

JoN CoRnYiN III (1952) BiN HoUstn, TX. Pop

AiR FrCe, MoVd ToKyo 1968. TrNty UniV

JoUnaLism, JD St MaRy UniV. LL.M ViGin sCH LaU

1998 TX ARrNy GeNaL, 2000 InTerNeT

BuReAu InVeTiGaTe iLleGaL PrAcTise. KriTzide

InVeSeTgAtE NiT TiMeLy BlAcS DrUg BuSt FaLs ArRst.

2002 rAn US SiNiT defeat DeMo boTh koSt 9 Mil

2008 reLect, 2014, 2020. CouRt HaUs VioLenCe

"jUdGs mAk PoLit dEsCiSoNs…UnAcCouNtabl"

May 2007 McKain yeLd pRoFaNiTy aT CoRnYiT,

AbT ImMiGrAtiOn. BiNgO KaRds mArK DeMo

JudiScArY CoMm SaID"FaR RiGhT" . VoT Against

ObMa SuPrm CrT. BLaM ChINa CoViD pAnDem,

oN RuSsaN iNtErfirAncE IN ElEcT hE QueStnd

FBI diReKtoR aBt HiLy CLiTiN VoT aGaInSt

StEm CeL FunD. AlLoW LaU eNf DNA sAmPl.

CoNsT AmEnd MaRag OnE mAn wO, VoT ReEsTatE

PaTriOt AkT, WiR TaPng. NeGaTv EfFeCt TarIFs.

VoT AgAiSt InDpiNd CoMm Jan 6 rIoT. ReP EsTaT TaX.

— *John Cornyn*

#44

LiNSeEd OLn GraHAM (1955) bOn SutH CaRliNa.

PaReN KaFe, IrSh-ScOt deSeNt. eNtrd

ReSvE OfFcir TrAing ScHoo, PaReN DiEd aT 21.

AtTenD UniV Suth CaRLin. BA psychology. LaU SChoo

AiRfoRcE defENc AtTorN. transfer FrAnkFrt, ChIEf

PrOsCuTor. On 60 Minuts deFnd PiLoT MarIjuna.

1989 priVt PrAc lAwyr in SutH CArLn. jOiNd

US AiRForC ReSeRv. 1990-91 aDviSd PiLoT.

2007 & 2009 WaR AdVsr. 1993-95 SC HauS Repr

1995-2003 US HaUs rEp. 1997 ImPeAvH INqUrY

CLiTMaN. 1998 aRTiKle of ImPeAcH.

GraHAM HaUs ImPeAcH manager. 2002 US SiNiT

2014 sUsPtbl PriMry ChALg beKauS CoMprMis DeMo

GraHAAM MacHiN, 2020 jUdCiA CoMmt Chr

2016 "IfF We NomAT DuMp wE will gEt DesTro"

In pReSd EleCt vOTd InDePd, nOt DuMp. 2019 SuPoRt

DuMp. MeT hIM. DuMp nOt RaCiSt, 'GraHAM'

DuMp should ChAlLgE 2020 ElEcTn. BuT

WhEn JaN 6 2021 ElEcTaL VotE 'BideN WuN'

— Lindsey Graham

#45

JoN RonDuLpH THorNe {1961} BrN PieR, Such DaK
PaP fighter PiLoT WW II. StAr AthLet,
BiOL UnIV, BasKetBaL. BA BusnEs. MBA BuSn Ad
LeGiS AiDe US SINiT 1985-87. 1991-93 RaLrD dR f GoV
1996 ELek US HaUs Rep. reLeK 2000, 2002.
US SiNiT 2005-pReSnt. 2004 RaSe DeFtd DAschL.
2018 kAlLd for EnD of RuSsan InVeStgt oF eLeKtn
dArY fArMrs MarGn CoV prOgm. DrUg
340B ProGrm, RePEeL EsTaTe TaX. EmPly
ParTiS AkT StUdNt LoAnS. FMCSA EXemPt
hEaT OiL TraNpOt SaFty ReG ShRtAg StTEmERgcy
VoTd AgAst GREEN DEAL. leTtR FaceBk anTi KoNsErvT
FaVord IrAq waR, MiLtRy command deCiDE.
AgAsT Nu START prOgM. MaSs ShOtiNg mUsT Pr-
tEk TheMslvs. UpDAte Norh AmEr FreE TrAD
AgRemnT. tRiF ProTeCt fArmR. DumP ATtcHe Hm
FoR niT vOTizng AGaiSt SerTiFd 2020 eLeKn
vOtD AGaisT InDeP CoMm jaN 6 Rizot. PosSblE
PreSidEntt KaNiTe. EVanGeLikAl XaiNt

— *John Thune*

46

MicHAiL DiNeSt RoGrs (1958) PoLi SciNce unDrgd
MasTr PuBlik AdmIn JaCk sT UniV. cLhUN CoMm
1994 AlBaM HaUs ReP. US HaUs ReP 2002.
reSeVed CaMpgn FuNds fr ARMPAC fr DeLy ConV
FeLny LaUnry Mony. noT reTrn. 2017-19 DePt of SpCe
Lau. AgGrsVe MiLitRy in Spac. TwN HaLl repeal
AfFoRdbl KaRe Akt. AsKd aBt CaMpgn ConTr
2021-22 JaN 6 "no PlAcE fiR PoliTkl ViOlAc. SuPrt
EffOrTs oVrtUn ElECtn. VoTd AgAnst ImPeC
voTd aGaSt Amekn ReCuE PlAn. RePs
VoTd AgAisT McKaRtY "TeRroRiSt". 14th BalLot
RoGrs LuNgD aT GaEtz, HUdsOn reStind Hm
lOckHeaD MarTin BiG CoNtrib tO RoGrs, hE AdVk
NGI miSsL prOg iN TiAwAn. AnT AbOrTin
VotD aGaISt VoLnCe AgAisT WumAn
2013. aGaiNsT eXpAnD hAte CriMeS. 2023 VoTd
FiSkAl reSpoNb Akt. AGaiSt JuN teeTh
sUpPt PAiTroT Akt. OnE oF 147 VoTd oVeR-
tuRn 2020 ElEctns. BaPtIst ChUrH.

— *Mike Rogers*

#47

JuN AnT BaRrAsSe III (1952) bOn ReDng PA.

CeN Cth HS ReNsellr PolYTeK, GeOrGTwN
UnIV BS BiOlgy. 1978 MD SChol oF Med. ReSiD-
eNty YaLe MdiKal. 1983 moVd WhYoMe
OrTHpedk pRaKic. StAt PreDnt MeDik SocIEty
roDEo PhyCiN. 1983-2007 sUrGn CaSpr
1996 losT US SiNiT rAcE. 2002 ELec WhYoMe
reELc 2006 trANsPt Hwy CoMm. 2007 goV
AppOiNt US SiNiT, 2008. reElct 2012, 2018.

"liMiTd GovMt, loWr TaX, lEsS sPnDng,
tRaD family VaLUe, LoKaL ConTtoL, sTr
NaTnaL DeFenCe. AnT AbOtin, 'A' rAt NaTRiF Asc
AgAiSt AFfoRbl HeAlh KaRe. diNy SciNt CoNc
CliMte ChAng. leTr DuMp enD PaRs aGrmnt.

AgNst ReForM oF FeDr prISn. FiRst StP aKt.
dUmP hAd nUmrus BuSsns Tys No RusSa inTerFr
OppOsd IMpeAch DuMp. AgAst 2023 FiScAl
rESpoNsbLy Akt. DiVorSe, PrEsbyTrIAn ChUR.

— John Barrasso III

DaNdi ALoNe WeBStiR (1949) 2011-preSnt HaUs
rEpSnT, US FL. 1980 fL hauS RePsnT 1998
FL. SiNiT. dIStNt ReLaTv OrAter. MvD FlOordA
SiNuS ReCoM. BS alEcTriK EnGeR. 1971.
SkIPd DrFit VieT WoR, PhySiKal, sTaNdng. Bekm
diSsTifIEd GovMnT, reJeCtd ZonINg. 1980
1982-1984 reELkd. FiRst BilL lAw
HuMe ScHoOl Akt 1985. CoVnT MarRgE.
FL SiNiT. TerM LiMt 2008. DrUg SteRod tEsTng HS.
AbORtn UlTrA sOUnd tEsTng. 2010 EntErd RaSe
US HaUs RePs. opposed LegIsLtn KlIMeT cHg
iNKrSe reVsNue. MisSd 5.5 of RoL kAlL vOts. StrE
LiNe GovMt. SpEnDng KuTs, FiNaSal reSpoN
drOp OuT US SiNiT rAse. HuMe EdKaTn
AlLoW coseLed wEpn. aGAist LGBT, sAmE sX
MaRAgE. OpPse AbORtn AlL SiRcUmstAnC. AgAiS
MeDiKal CaNnBis in rEdEnSe. tAX CuT
& JoB Akt 2017. siGNd LuW SuiTe koNtEst
PiNnsylva & TXaSs. MeDikaL ObL ImPc

— Daniel Webster

#49

JuN NeEL KiNnEd (1951) brN MiSsPi

gRaD VanDrBLt & uNiV VirGin LaUw

MagDaL CoLg OxFrD. 1999 stAt TrEasR reEktd

2003….2007. uNsCesSfL SiNiT 2004, 2008

SwiCtd PaRti 2007 beKam REPUB, 2017 raN DeF

DeMo, 2020 oBjTd ArZoNa PreZidt eLect

reLkd 2002 US SiNiT. 2017 juNe grILd SeCtaY Ed

'yoUng PuPiLs in RuRL ArReA neeD ChOiC

'siX MayOnASe in OvRpRsD CaP stOr'

KroSd PArtY LinE vOtD aGaInSt 3 SuPrM cRt

NoMny. inTrDuCd 'FoRgN HolDg KoMpy AKoknt

AkT. 2020 VotD aMy ConEy SuPrm CrT

2020 PrEZ eLctn. OjKtd sErtn sTAtes ELecTL

VoT. Jan 6 RiOtrs "jAiL" BiDen SiGnd

hiS DUMP OpiOiD Akt. 2022 VoTd aGaISt KeJeNi

BrN JaCKsn SUPMe CrT. QuizZd BjzeLkeNgr

juDiSaL NomIneE sTAtE LegISLT & CoNsTutOn.

MaY 2023 "wIThOut PePL US, MeXcO

EAtNG Kat FoOd Out KanS, LiVng TeNtS".

— John Kennedy

DoNeL W NoRcHriSt (1958) BorN CaMdeN, NJ

ApPendSt InTnT ELeCt WoRkrs. 3 brOthErs

RaiSed in PeEnSaUkn TwP. CaMdeN Couny CoL

degree CrIm justice. AttEnD RuTgErs UniV.

LuThERn FaItH. 16 yrs AFL-CIO CenRL LaBoR coUc

EleCt NJ AsSmbLy 2009. ApPoiNt SiNiT

NJ 2010, 2011, 2013, reEleTd. 2014 EnDORs

By DeMo MaChINe. oNLi Safe DeMo

DisTrk in SuD New Jerzip. ElecTd 2014. He

WaS SlanDErd whL oN ZooM lAbOr &

EduKatn CoMmti. hIS BrOth GeOrg DeMo LeaDr

BusNismAn. JoH PsyChiSt . LiV cAmdn.

— *Donald Norcross*

Printed in the USA
CPSIA information can be obtained
at www.ICGtesting.com
LVHW092152311023
762731LV00031B/287